WORLDS AND LIVES

AN ESSAY WRITING GUIDE FOR GCSE (9-1)

R. P. DAVIS

Published by Accolade Tuition Ltd
71-75 Shelton Street
Covent Garden
London WC2H 9JQ
www.accoladetuition.com
info@accoladetuition.com

ISBN 978-1-913988-40-1

FIRST EDITION
1 3 5 7 9 10 8 6 4 2

CONTENTS

FOREWORD

In your GCSE English Literature exam, you will be presented with a single poem from the *Worlds and Lives* anthology and a question that invites you to compare and contrast this poem with one other anthology poem of your choosing. Of course, there are many methods one *might* use to tackle this style of question. However, there is one particular technique which, due to its sophistication, most readily allows students to unlock the highest marks: namely, **the thematic method**.

To be clear, this study guide is *not* intended to walk you through the poems line-by-line: there are many great guides out there that do just that. No, this guide, by sifting through a series of mock exam questions, will demonstrate *how* to organise a response thematically and thus write a stellar essay: a skill we believe no other study guide adequately covers!

I have encountered students who have structured their essays all sorts of ways: some by writing about one or both of the poems line-by-line, others by identifying various language techniques and giving each its own paragraph. The method I'm advocating, on the other hand, involves picking out three themes that will allow you to holistically answer the question: these three themes will become the three content paragraphs of your essay, cushioned between a brief introduction and conclusion. Ideally, these themes will follow from one to the next to create a flowing argument. Within each of these thematic paragraphs, you can then ensure you are jumping through the mark scheme's hoops.

So to break things down further, each thematic paragraph will include various point-scoring components. In each paragraph, you will quote from the poem the exam board has set, offer analyses of these quotes, then discuss how the specific language techniques you have identified illustrate the theme you're discussing. In each paragraph, you will then quote from the second poem (the one you've chosen to write on), and, while analysing these quotes and remarking on language techniques, also explain not only how the second poem relates to the chosen theme, but also how it does so differently (or not!) from the first poem.

Don't worry if this all feels daunting. Throughout this guide, I will be illustrating in great detail – by means of examples – how to build an essay of this kind.

Haworth, Yorkshire. This is likely the sort of natural vista Emily Brontë was envisaging in 'Shall earth no more inspire thee'.

The beauty of the thematic approach is that, once you have your themes, you suddenly have a direction and a trajectory, and this makes essay writing a whole lot easier. However, it must also be noted that extracting themes in the first place is something students often find tricky. I have come across many candidates who understand the poems inside out; but when they are presented with a question under exam conditions, and the pressure kicks in, they find it tough to break their response down into themes. The fact of the matter is: the process is a *creative* one and the best themes require a bit of imagination.

In this guide, I shall take nine different exam-style questions, and put together nine essay plans that ensure that every poem in the anthology is discussed in depth at least once. These essay plans will also be accompanied by notes illustrating how we will be satisfying the mark scheme's criteria. Please do keep in mind that, when operating under timed conditions, your plans will necessarily be less detailed than those that appear in this volume.

A mural in Minneapolis, USA, for George Floyd. After Floyd's murder at the hands of a police officer in 2020, there came an outpouring of protest and artistic expression. Police profiling is also at the heart of Caleb Femi's poem, 'Thirteen'.

Before I move forward in earnest, I believe it to be worthwhile to run through the four Assessment Objectives the exam board want you to cover in your response – if only to demonstrate how effective the thematic response can be. I would argue that the first Assessment Objective (AO1) – the one that wants candidates to 'read, understand and respond to texts' and which is worth 12 of the total 30 marks up for grabs – will be wholly satisfied by selecting strong themes, then fleshing them out with quotes. Indeed, when it comes to identifying the top-scoring candidates for AO1, the mark scheme explicitly tells examiners to look for a 'critical, exploratory, conceptualised response' that makes 'judicious use of precise references' – the word 'concept' is a synonym of theme, and 'judicious references' simply refers to quotes that appropriately support the theme you've chosen.

The second Assessment Objective (AO2) – which is also responsible for 12 marks – asks students to 'analyse the language, form and structure used by a writer to create meanings and effects, using relevant subject terminology where appropriate.' As noted, you will already be quoting from the poems as you back up your themes, and it is a natural progression to then analyse the language techniques used. In fact, this is far more effective than simply observing language techniques (personification here, alliteration there), because by discussing how the language techniques relates to and shapes the theme, you will also be demonstrating how the writer 'create[s] meanings and effects.'

Now, in my experience, language analysis is the most important element of AO2 – perhaps 8 of the 12 marks will go towards language analysis. You will also notice, however, that AO2 asks students to comment on 'form and structure.' Again, the thematic approach has your back – because though simply shoehorning in a point on form or structure will feel jarring, when you bring these points up while discussing a theme, as a means to further a thematic argument, you will again organically be discussing the way it 'create[s] meanings and effects.'

AO3 requires you to 'show understanding of the relationships between texts and the contexts in which they were written' and is responsible for a more modest 6 marks in total. These are easy enough to weave into a thematic argument; indeed, the theme gives the student a chance to bring up context in a relevant and fitting way. After all, you don't want it to look like you've just shoehorned a contextual factoid into the mix.

Finally, you have AO4 – known also as 'spelling and grammar.' Technically speaking, there are no AO4 marks up for grabs in this particular section of the paper. That said, I would still suggest that you take care on this front. The examiners are human beings, and if you are demonstrating a strong grasp of spelling and grammar, most examiners (whether rightly or wrongly!) will still be more inclined to mark your paper more generously.

My hope is that this book, by demonstrating how to tease out themes from a pair of poems, will help you feel more confident in doing so yourself. I believe it is also worth mentioning that the themes I have picked out are by no means definitive. Asked the very same question, someone else may pick out different themes, and write an answer that is just as good (if not better!). Obviously the exam is not likely to be fun – my memory of them is pretty much the exact opposite. But still, this is one of the very few chances that you will get at GCSE level to actually be creative. And to my mind at least, that was always more enjoyable – if *enjoyable* is the right word – than simply demonstrating that I had memorised loads of facts.

You'd be surprised how cheaply you can get hold of poetry these days!

ESSAY PLAN ONE
'LINES WRITTEN IN EARLY SPRING' & 'WITH BIRDS YOU'RE NEVER LONELY'

Lines Written in Early Spring
By William Wordsworth

I heard a thousand blended notes,
While in a grove I sate reclined,
In that sweet mood when pleasant thoughts
Bring sad thoughts to the mind.

To her fair works did Nature link
The human soul that through me ran;
And much it grieved my heart to think
What man has made of man.

Through primrose tufts, in that green bower,
The periwinkle trailed its wreaths;
And 'tis my faith that every flower
Enjoys the air it breathes.

The birds around me hopped and played,

Their thoughts I cannot measure:—
But the least motion which they made
It seemed a thrill of pleasure.

The budding twigs spread out their fan,
To catch the breezy air;
And I must think, do all I can,
That there was pleasure there.

If this belief from heaven be sent,
If such be Nature's holy plan,
Have I not reason to lament
What man has made of man?

Compare the ways in which the poets convey the relationship between humanity and nature in 'Lines Written in Early Spring' by William Wordsworth and one other poem from Worlds and Lives.

Introduction

I have opted to invoke 'With Birds You're Never Lonely' by Raymond Antrobus for this particular comparison, as both poems deal with the interplay between humanity and nature. My philosophy is that your introduction ought to be doing two things. First, it should be scoring early AO3 points by placing the poems in context. Second, it should be giving a hint as to where your discussion is heading, since, by doing so, you are allowing the examiner to gain their bearings and thus ready themselves to award you AO1 marks.

'While Wordsworth's 'Composed Upon Westminster Bridge' presents an idyllic depiction of the harmony between civilisation and nature in the heart of London, 'Lines Written in Early Spring' delves into the dichotomy between the beauty and harmony of nature and the destructive tendencies of mankind.[1] In this essay, we will explore the connection between humanity and nature in 'Lines Written in Early Spring' and contrast it with Raymond Antrobus's 'With Birds You're Never Lonely,' which also examines the emotional impact of the natural world and the potential for a more harmonious relationship between humans and their environment.'

Theme/Paragraph One: By delving into the minute beauty of the natural world, both poems convey the profound emotional impact nature is capable of having on mankind — the sheer amount of detail in both implicitly gestures to their fascination.

- In Wordsworth's poem, the speaker's observations of the 'thousand blended notes' and 'primrose tufts' in the grove highlight the detailed beauty of the natural world. The poem's iambic tetrameter, with its steady and rhythmic pulse, mimics the natural ebb and flow of the speaker's emotions, creating a sense of harmony within the poem.[2] This metrical structure allows the words to flow gently, drawing readers into the speaker's emotional connection with the natural world. The phrase 'thousand blended notes' evokes a sense of unity and harmony among the various elements, emphasising the richness and diversity present in nature. The vibrant, sensory imagery of the 'primrose tufts' and 'periwinkle trail[ing] its wreaths' illustrates the visual appeal of the grove. These instances of detailed observation indicate the speaker's deep appreciation and fascination with nature, drawing readers to admire the beauty around them. [*AO1 for judiciously selecting quotes and advancing the argument; AO2 for discussing scansion and how form shapes meaning*]

- *Pivot to comparison*: In Antrobus's poem, the speaker also vividly depicts the beauty of the natural world, describing the 'sun-syrupped Kauri trees' and 'brazen Tui birds' in the Zelandia forest. The use of alliteration in 'sun-syrupped' creates a harmonious and rich tone, suggesting warmth and abundance. The personification of the 'brazen Tui birds,' with their boldness and audacity, highlights the speaker's admiration for the creatures and the emotional impact nature has on him. [*AO2 for close language analysis and techniques*]
- Both poets, then, convey the idea that humans can find solace and emotional resonance in the intricate details of nature. Their shared focus on these minute, beautiful aspects of the natural world reinforces the deep emotional power nature holds for mankind. [*AO1 for comparison*]

Theme/Paragraph Two: Both poems set up a dichotomy between the harmony of nature and a version of mankind that stands in contrast.

- In Wordsworth's poem, the phrase 'what man has made of man' employs metonymy to highlight humanity's harsh and destructive tendencies – tendencies that stand in stark contrast to the harmoniousness of nature.[3] The first instance of 'man' stands for those individuals in society responsible for actions or decisions, while the second 'man' represents humanity as a whole. Together, this phrase expresses how human actions have negatively impacted society at large. Indeed, given that the poem was written during a period characterised by significant violence, upheaval, and exploitation (the French Revolution and the Industrial Revolution were both reverberating across the globe), this line serves as Wordsworth's critique of these societal transformations. [*AO1 for judiciously selecting quotes; AO2 for close analysis of the literary technique; AO3 for historical context*]
- Pivot to comparison: Antrobus's poem also portrays a division between the harmony of nature and the sterility of human civilisation, as seen in the café setting. The cacophony of noises caused by the 'barista' and the slamming of 'spoons' starkly contrasts with the peacefulness of the forest setting. He further explores this dichotomy through his discussion of hearing aids, which represent a piece of modern technology that acts as a barrier between himself and the natural world. In rejecting the use of the hearing aid while in nature, the speaker contemplates the possibility of a more harmonious connection with his surroundings. [*AO1 for advancing the argument judiciously selected quotes*]

Theme/Paragraph Three: In spite of their awareness that mankind falls short, both poems posit a kind of hopeful vision of a more harmonious connection between mankind and nature.

- In Wordsworth's poem, the speaker expresses a belief in 'Nature's holy plan,' which implies an underlying hope for mankind to eventually find harmony with nature and fulfil its potential for living in accordance with its surroundings. The use of religious language in 'holy plan' adds a sense of reverence and awe to the speaker's belief — while the structural choice to rhyme the word 'plan' with 'man' at the end of the poem optimistically intertwines humanity with this divine guidance. This idea reflects the Romantic ideal of finding solace and redemption in nature, and also gestures to Wordsworth's deeply held pantheistic beliefs.[4] [*AO1 for judiciously selecting quotes; AO2 for close language analysis and for discussing how structure shapes meaning; AO3 for historical context*]
- *Pivot to comparison*: Antrobus's poem presents a similar hope for a more harmonious connection between mankind and nature, as illustrated through the speaker's encounter with the Maori woman and her teachings about birds.[5] This cultural exchange provides the speaker with an alternative perspective on nature, suggesting that adopting different ways of understanding and engaging with the natural world can lead to greater harmony. The inclusion of the proverb '*with birds you're never lonely*' — which is italicised in the poem for emphasis — captures a

poignant sentiment that highlights the significance of finding a connection with nature. [*AO1 for judiciously selecting quotes; AO2 for close analysis; AO3 for historical context*]

- Despite their different historical and personal contexts, both poets encourage readers to explore the potential for a more harmonious connection between mankind and nature. Through their depictions of hope and the transformative power of the natural world, they challenge readers to reflect on their own relationships with nature and consider its emotional impact.

Conclusion:

There is no set way to tackle the conclusion. Sometimes I'll have an extra mini theme up my sleeve, and in that case I'll integrate it into the conclusion to satisfy AO1 criteria. It can also be a good opportunity to score some extra AO3 (historical context) marks, as I have done here. I suppose the key thing, as you are wrapping things up, is to ensure you keep one eye on the assessment objectives.

'Interestingly, Antrobus was born with partial deafness; and, in an interview with NPR in 2022, he reflected how, at a music festival, he was forced to remove his earpiece and sit in 'not quite silence, but a kind of quieter, muffled kind of sound.' With his ambivalence towards the device that helps him mediate the stimuli of the external world, Antrobus gestures towards a common theme in both poems — the desire to connect with nature, and yet a cautiousness towards the human trappings that complicate mankind's relationship with the natural world.'[6]

The Peak District, the slice of England where William Wordsworth grew up

ESSAY PLAN TWO
'A PORTABLE PARADISE' & 'SHALL EARTH NO MORE INSPIRE THEE'

Shall earth no more inspire thee
By Emily Brontë

Shall earth no more inspire thee,
Thou lonely dreamer now?
Since passion may not fire thee
Shall Nature cease to bow?

Thy mind is ever moving
In regions dark to thee;
Recall its useless roving—
Come back and dwell with me.

I know my mountain breezes
Enchant and soothe thee still—
I know my sunshine pleases
Despite thy wayward will.

When day with evening blending
Sinks from the summer sky,

I've seen thy spirit bending
In fond idolatry.

I've watched thee every hour;
I know my mighty sway,
I know my magic power
To drive thy griefs away.

Few hearts to mortals given
On earth so wildly pine;
Yet none would ask a heaven
More like this earth than thine.

Then let my winds caress thee;
Thy comrade let me be—
Since nought beside can bless thee,
Return and dwell with me.

Discuss the theme of solace in 'Shall earth no more inspire thee' by Emily Brontë and one other poem from Worlds and Lives.

Introduction

On this occasion, I've decided to bring in Roger Robinson's 'A Portable Paradise'. Again, notice how I start by quickly scoring AO3 marks for context, then start hinting at the thematic gist of my essay in order to pick up early AO1 marks.

'In a June 2020 interview with *The Guardian*, Roger Robinson poignantly described poems as 'empathy machines.' Extending this metaphor, one can see Robinson's 'A Portable Paradise' and Emily Brontë's 'Shall earth no more inspire thee' as not just conduits of empathy, but also as vehicles for exploring and offering solace. Divergent in their cultural and historical contexts, both works illuminate the shared human longing for solace, fuelled by the nostalgia-laden allure of the natural world.'

Theme/Paragraph One: Solace is found in the natural world. In Brontë's poem, the speaker *is* nature, and, according to nature's own narrative, its realm has given its interlocutor solace and happiness.[1] In Robinson's piece, the exact nature of the portable paradise he carries is unclear — yet it is likened metaphorically to the natural world. As such, the natural world figures as a source of solace, albeit at a metaphorical remove.

- In Robinson's poem, the portable paradise, though abstract, is distilled into tangible, sensory experiences through the use of synecdoche.[2] This figure of speech, where a part represents the whole, allows the vastness of the natural world to be condensed into a compact form. When he writes, 'trace its ridges in your pocket, smell its piney scent on your handkerchief,' each experience — the tactile sensation of tracing ridges and olfactory scent of pine — are parts that evoke the whole of nature as a paradise. In using synecdoche, Robinson turns abstract paradise into a sensory experience, hence spotlighting the role of language in creating personal paradises that provide solace. [*AO1 for advancing the argument with a judiciously selected quote; AO2 for discussing how synecdoche shapes meaning in the poem*]

- <u>*Pivot to comparison*</u>: Resonating with the Romantic ethos, Brontë's poem lavishes in the enchanting allure of the natural world offering solace and inspiration. The poem personifies nature, and employs anaphora, as seen in phrases like 'I know my mountain breezes enchant' and 'I know my sunshine pleases', to emphasise nature's relentlessness in providing comfort.[3] This could also reflect Brontë's personal longing: the Brontë sisters, Emily included, were known for their deep emotional connection to the rugged landscapes around their home in Haworth, Yorkshire. Understanding Brontë's own deep-rooted connection to nature lends additional resonance to this plea from the poem's speaker. [*AO1 for advancing the argument with a judiciously selected quote; AO2 for discussing the use of anaphora, and thus how form shapes meaning. AO3 for placing the poem within the Romantic movement & linking it to Brontë's biography*]
- The poets, then, contrast in their use of nature. Robinson, through synecdoche and metaphor, likens the abstract idea of personal solace to elements of nature, creating a 'portable paradise.' The implicated natural world is not physically present but serves as a symbol for peace and comfort. On the other hand, for

Brontë's speaker, it is the literal natural world itself that is the source of solace and comfort.

Theme/Paragraph Two: In Brontë's poem, there is a sense that the interlocutor has become detached from the natural world as a source of solace — the poem is a clarion call for the interlocutor to reengage and seek solace once more.[4] Yet if Brontë's poem deals with someone who has strayed from a source of solace, Robinson's, by contrast, deals with a speaker who hoards his source of solace at all times. The instability is not that the speaker will stray from the pocket paradise, but that someone might steal it.

- Brontë's poem embodies a regretful tone, using melodious iambic meter to convey the peace and tranquility of nature, while also underlining the interlocutor's straying from it. The oscillation between stressed and unstressed syllables in the line 'Recall its useless roving' mimics the organic rhythm of natural elements, invoking longing to return.[5] [*AO1 for advancing the argument with a judiciously selected quote; AO2 for analysing scansion and tone*]
- *Pivot to comparison*: In Robinson's poem, the speaker's apprehension manifests through strategic enjambment, reverberating the undercurrent of unease as he navigates the tumultuous world. [6]One of the ways Robinson does this is by separating the phrase 'on my person,' at the end of one line, with 'concealed,' at the start of the next. This separation of two parts of the same image not only imitates the

hidden nature of the 'paradise,' but also captures the speaker's cautious mentality. Furthermore, phrases like 'concealed, so / no one else would know but me' feature a line break after 'so' — this break heightens not only the suspense of the phrases but also the speaker's sense of precariousness.[7] His 2020 Guardian interview reveals Robinson's experiences with the 'pressure and despair of trying to survive,' which reinforces the speaker's almost desperate desire to stow away his portable paradise intact and hidden. This careful use of enjambment lends a structural mirroring to the poem, further marking the correlation between the speaker's guarded mindset and his need for solace amid external threats. [*AO1 for advancing the argument with a judiciously selected quote; AO2 for analysing structural features; AO3 for connecting the poem to the poet's personal outlook as reflected in his interview*]

Theme/Paragraph Three: Both poems posit an elder protector as the source of solace. In Robinson's poem, it is the grandmother — the font of wisdom. In Brontë's poem, it is mother nature herself — a kind of personified elder protector.

- Significantly, in Robinson's poem, the speaker imbues his grandmother with the ethereal quality of the 'paradise.'[8] The lines 'And if I speak of Paradise, / then I'm speaking of my grandmother,' subtly link the notion of a paradisiacal abode to the figure of his grandmother, thus transforming a traditionally celestial entity — 'Paradise' — into a tangible figure —

the speaker's 'grandmother'.[9] By embedding the metaphor of 'paradise' within the person of the grandmother, Robinson beautifully encapsulates the essence of solace garnered from familial ties. The metaphor serves as an intimate emblem of solace, further exemplifying the individualised nature of comfort [*AO1 for advancing the argument with a judiciously selected quote; AO2 for analysing the metaphorical link established*]

- *Pivot to comparison*: In Brontë's poem, nature takes the role of the protector, nurturing the 'lonely dreamer' back to her bosom. The line 'I know my magic power' employs hyperbole – an exaggerated claim of nature's power symbolising its magnanimity in offering comfort.[10] [*AO1 for advancing the argument with a judiciously selected quote; AO2 for discussing the use of hyperbole*]
- Both poems, then, use protectors and their associated wisdom as anchors of solace. Robinson's emphasises the passed-down wisdom of the grandmother, while Brontë's hyperbole nurtures a magnanimous picture of the natural world.

Conclusion

As you may already know, AO3 marks can be won by invoking other relevant texts – texts that might not be in your syllabus, but nevertheless help enrich our understanding of the texts under scrutiny. As such, I have made a quick reference to Toni Morrison's novel *Beloved* in my conclusion, thereby ensuring that my AO3 bases are covered.

'A Portable Paradise' and 'Shall earth no more inspire thee' adroitly transmit a universal quest for solace. Robinson champions the role of familial wisdom in building personal paradises of solace is reminiscent of the enduring character of Baby Suggs in Toni Morrison's *Beloved*, who embodied wisdom and solace amid adversity. Brontë, resonating with Romantic ideals, perceives solace in the throes of nature, particularly through an ongoing plea for reconnection.'

A painting of Emily Brontë by her brother, Patrick Branwell Brontë.

ESSAY PLAN THREE
'ON AN AFTERNOON TRAIN FROM PURLEY TO VICTORIA, 1955' & 'NAME JOURNEYS'

A portrait of James Berry. We have opted not to reproduce Berry's poem in full: it is still in copyright and we wish to respect that fact.

Compare the ways in which the poets explore feelings of displacement and dislocation in 'On an Afternoon Train from Purley to Victoria, 1955' by James Berry and one other poem from Worlds and Lives.

Introduction

AO3 can be as simple as alluding to events from an author's life that might give insight into their work. Indeed, this is the approach I've taken in my introduction below...

> 'Before gaining recognition as a poet, James Berry worked in various industries, including as a telegraph operator and a dental technician, providing him with numerous opportunities to observe and experience the challenges of immigrant life in Britain. These experiences would later give rise to powerful, evocative works like 'On an Afternoon Train from Purley to Victoria, 1955,' which captures the complexities of displacement and adaptation faced by Caribbean migrants. In a similar vein, Raman Mundair's 'Name Journeys' delves into the emotional dislocation experienced by South Asian immigrants in Britain, offering an intimate exploration of the struggles they face in adapting to their new environment.'

Theme/Paragraph One: Both poems allude to diverse geographical locations in order to emphasise the speaker's sense of dislocation.

- In Mundair's poem, the speaker herself engages in a straightforward juxtaposition between her native land and her new home in Britain — the difference inspires a feeling of profound displacement.[1] The poem's speaker contrasts the richness of their Indian and Punjabi heritage, symbolised by the 'infinite silk' of the sari and the 'banyan leaves with sugar cane,' with the 'infertile English soil' that now surrounds her. [*AO1 for advancing the argument with judiciously selected quotes*]

- In Mundair's 2020 essay, 'Being In Process and Inertia,' Mundair reflects on her personal struggles with adjusting to a new environment – feeling 'cold' even when it is warm, and feeling constantly exhausted. This sense of always feeling out of place, and never quite at home, is echoed in the poem through the comparison of the speaker's Indian and Punjabi heritage with the 'infertile English soil'. [*AO3 for contextualising the poem within Mundair's personal experiences and her essay*]
- Pivot to comparison: In Berry's poem, however, it is the Quaker the speaker encounters that yokes two vastly different locations, under the mistaken idea that Jamaica and Africa are synonymous – 'What part of Africa is Jamaica? she said'. Indeed, the lack of speech marks in this line subtly telegraphs that the woman's ignorance is inseparable from her identity; and it is this ignorance of places populated by people of colour, while perhaps not malicious, that induces a sense of displacement in the poem's narrator. [*AO1 for advancing the argument with judiciously selected quotes; AO2 for discussing how form shapes meaning*]
- The Quaker's conflation of Jamaica and Africa reveals not only her ignorance of the speaker's true homeland, but also a larger misunderstanding of the diversity within cultures populated by people of colour. The

speaker artfully corrects the Quaker's error by acknowledging the contrast of cultural backgrounds, half-jokingly associating Jamaica's location with 'where Ireland is near Lapland.' This interaction emphasises the differences between the speaker and the Quaker, as well as the speaker's feelings of displacement in Britain. [*AO1 for advancing the argument with a judiciously selected quote; AO3 for contextualising the poem within the Windrush Generation*]

Theme Paragraph Two: In both poems, interactions with the anglicised world enhance the sense of dislocation.

- In Mundair's poem, the speaker posits the nameless, faceless Mancunians who, with their 'English mouths', strip the lyricism from her name and cannibalise her culture. The poem deploys the literary technique of synecdoche to highlight the significance of the speaker's name as a representative of her entire cultural identity. Her name, which has become 'dislodged' among their new English-speaking community, stands as a symbol for the many ways in which the speaker's South Asian heritage is being eroded and distorted in her new surroundings. By concentrating the themes of displacement and adaptation within this single aspect of the speaker's experience, Mundair effectively conveys the challenges faced by South Asian migrants in Britain. [*AO1 for advancing the argument with a judiciously selected quote; AO2 for discussing how the literary technique of synecdoche enriches meaning; AO3 for contextualising the poem within South Asian migration to Britain*]

- In Berry's poem, the Quaker, induces ambivalence: her focus on race and 'racial brotherhood', while borne from sincerity and goodness, only serves to remind the speaker of his otherness in British society. Although her sincerity is described as 'beautiful,' the speaker's encounter with her reminds him of the cultural and geographical chasms that separate them, exacerbating his feelings of displacement amid British society wrestling with multiculturalism. [*AO1 for advancing the argument with a judiciously selected quote; AO3 for contextualising the poem within the Windrush Generation and British society*]

Theme Paragraph Three: The intensity of their memories of the world from which they originate sharpens the sense of dislocation in both poems: even though they are physically in the West, their minds are elsewhere, creating a sense of dislocation.

- In Mundair's poem, the mythology associated with the culture from which she hails continues to loom large in her imagination – a presence that always reminds her of her displacement. Mundair's piece evokes the images of Rama, Sita, and the alliterative 'sari sisters' from Indian mythology, drawing on the power of cultural memory to anchor the speaker in their native identity even while they experience displacement in Britain. The poem emphasises the role of mythology in shaping the speaker's self-understanding and underscores the distance between her native heritage and her adopted culture. [*AO1 for advancing the argument with a judiciously selected quote; AO2 for discussing how language shapes meaning; AO3 for contextualising the poem within South Asian culture and migration to Britain*]

- *Pivot to comparison*: In Berry's poem, the speaker's sudden and inexplicable remembrance of Jamaica contributes to the feeling of dislocation. In Berry's poem, the speaker's recollection of his father's 'big banana field' is conveyed through an irregular metre (anapestic feet mixed with iambs), which contrasts sharply with the more regular iambic metre used throughout the rest of the poem.[2] This striking metrical deviation mirrors the sense of disconnection or dislocation the speaker feels within his new environment, as he remembers the familiar rhythm of life back in Jamaica. This point demonstrates the poet's skilful use of scansion to reinforce themes of displacement and cultural difference in the poem. [*AO1 for advancing the argument with a judiciously selected quote; AO2 for discussing how scansion and form shapes meaning; AO3 for contextualising the poem within the Windrush Generation*]

Conclusion:

'Berry and Mundair both adeptly explore feelings of displacement and adaptation through their respective poems, capturing the emotional complexities experienced by Caribbean and South Asian migrants as they navigate life in post-war Britain. By engaging with themes of cultural difference, encounters with anglicised society, and memories of their native lands, both poets powerfully convey the challenges faced by individuals grappling with the dual realities of maintaining their origins while adapting to new environments.'

ESSAY PLAN FOUR

'A CENTURY LATER' & 'THIRTEEN'

Malala Yousafzai's protest against the Taliban is powerfully dramatised in Imtiaz Dharker's 'A Century Later'. We have opted not to reproduce Dharker's poem in full: it is still in copyright and we wish to respect that fact.

Explore the ideas of rebellion and resistance in 'A Century Later' by Imtiaz

Dharker and one other poem from Worlds and Lives.

Introduction

Here I have decided to compare the ideas of rebellion and resistance in Imtiaz Dharker's 'A Century Later' and Caleb Femi's 'Thirteen.' Although both poems deal with young individuals who face oppressive forces, they explore resistance in different ways. Dharker's poem emphasises the significance of education as a form of rebellion, while Femi's piece highlights the power of memory and identity in resisting oppressive systems and stereotypes.

> 'In George Schuyler's 1931 novel, *Black No More*, the Black protagonist, in a surreal act of both surrender and rebellion, takes advantage of a technology that renders him Caucasian in appearance, then proceeds to subvert the KKK from within.[1] For Femi's Black protagonist in 'Thirteen', however, no such science-fiction option exists; instead, the protagonist, in the face of police profiling, is left to rely on the power of memory to attempt to resist. By contrast, in Dharker's 'A Century Later' – a fictionalised account of a girl's defiance influenced by the real-life story of Malala Yousafzai – it is the pursuit of education that figures as the pivotal mechanism for resistance and rebellion.'[2]

Theme/Paragraph One: Both poems illustrate the context of adversity and oppression that their

protagonists face. In 'A Century Later,' a young girl confronts the threat of violence due to her pursuit of education, while in 'Thirteen,' a Black teenage boy faces racial profiling and police brutality.

- In Dharker's poem, the use of spondees in the opening lines, with their stressed syllables, helps emphasise the intensity of a 'battle' and 'firing-line' that the girl confronts while seeking an education.[3] The spondees create a heavier, oppressive rhythm, reflecting the daughter's struggle within a society that seeks to control and limit her education, mirroring the challenges faced by girls like Malala Yousafzai in regions where the Taliban has an influence.[4] [*AO1 for advancing the argument with judiciously selected quotes; AO2 for discussing how scansion and form enriches meaning; AO3 for placing the poem in historical context*]
- Pivot to comparison: In Femi's 'Thirteen,' the titular age of the protagonist underscores his vulnerability in the face of oppressive law enforcement. The final line of the opening stanza — 'Thirteen, you'll tell him: you're thirteen' — is particularly potent: not only does the repetition of 'thirteen' convey a compelling incredulity, but the use of 'you'll' and 'you're' reaffirms the second person narrative technique that puts the reader vicariously in the shoes of the detainee, forcing them to confront the ugliness of the situation. [*AO1 for advancing the argument with judiciously selected quotes; AO2 for discussing how language and structure shapes meaning*]

- This abrupt encounter with an officer stands in stark contrast to the innocent, hopeful memory of a younger version of the protagonist hearing about 'supernovas' in school from the very same officer. That this officer first appeared at the protagonist's primary school ('Gloucester Primary School') adds another layer of irony — this officer is also a part-time educator, and thus ought to know better. It is perhaps unsurprising that this poem first appeared in November 2020 — its publication came just six months after the murder of George Floyd in the U.S. city of Minneapolis, an event that supercharged the Black Lives Movement, and heightened awareness across the Western world of police profiling.[5] [*AO1 for advancing the argument with judiciously selected quotes; AO3 for placing the poem in historical context*]
- Both poems, then, depict young people who are unfairly targeted and facing a dangerous reality due to societal circumstances beyond their control.

Theme/Paragraph Two: Each poem explores the power of resistance and rebellion against the oppressive forces faced by the protagonists. In 'A Century Later,' the girl's unwavering pursuit of education represents defiance, while in 'Thirteen,' the protagonist's attempt to recall a shared memory with the officer serves as an act of resistance.

- Dharker's poem dramatises the girl's resistance against the 'bullet' as she bravely declares, 'you are stupid.' The girl's defiance, in her determination to attend school and continue learning, demonstrates the power of knowledge in challenging and overcoming oppressive forces. This act of rebellion can be seen as part of a larger historical push for women's rights and education in regions where they have been historically restricted, such as Pakistan, Afghanistan, and other areas under the influence of extremist groups. [*AO1 for advancing the argument with judiciously selected quotes; AO3 for placing the poem in historical context*]

- *Pivot to comparison*: In 'Thirteen,' the protagonist's attempt to remind the officer of their shared past and their once-inspiring words about 'supernovas' serves as an act of resistance. With his simple plea, 'Don't you remember me?', the protagonist seeks to disrupt and counteract the oppressive racial narrative imposed upon him by the officers. Moreover, by invoking the symbolism of the supernova that the officer himself has originally used when visiting their school – the officer had told the children that they 'were all *supernovas*' – the protagonist resists by reminding us of his shared humanity: all humans are, after all, the products of stardust. This approach is reminiscent of influential autobiographical works such as Maya Angelou's 'I Know Why the Caged Bird Sings,' in which memory and personal experience are used to challenge discrimination and empower marginalised individuals.[6] [*AO1 for advancing the argument with judiciously selected quotes; AO2 for close language analysis; AO3 for referencing a third text and placing the poem in a larger artistic and historical context*]

- Both protagonists, then, through their acts of rebellion and resistance, force a confrontation with the oppressive forces in their respective environments.

Theme/Paragraph Three: Additionally, both poems convey the impact of resistance and rebellion, particularly in inspiring others or potentially changing perceptions.

- In 'A Century Later,' Dharker employs hyperbole in describing the impact of the girl's determination to continue her education in the face of violence. When she says that 'the schoolgirls are standing up / to take their places on the front line,' the hyperbolic imagery of a military front line elevates the girls' collective act of resistance, equating their pursuit of education with an act of bravery. [*AO1 for advancing the argument with judiciously selected quotes; AO2 for close language analysis*]
- The poem also uses meta-fictionality to emphasise the impact of the girl's act of resistance: when the speaker asserts that 'You cannot kill a book / or the buzzing in it', it draws our attention to the fact that the poem we are reading is itself a work of literature — a 'buzzing' instance of defiance inspired by an act of defiance.[7] Dharker herself, with her poem, is standing shoulder to shoulder with the 'schoolgirls' in the 'front line'. [*AO1 for advancing the argument with judiciously selected quotes; AO2 for close language analysis*]
- *Pivot to comparison*: Femi's 'Thirteen' offers a more ambiguous outcome, as it remains unclear whether the officer will remember the shared past and

change his treatment of the protagonist. By confronting the officer with his memories, the protagonist attempts to create an alternative to the stereotype with which he is being unfairly targeted. However, at the close of the poem, the protagonist recalls a second memory — his teacher informing him supernovas 'are, in fact, dying stars/ on the verge of becoming black holes'. With these lines, supernovas suddenly cease to be symbols of shared humanity; instead, they are recast as bleak symbols of death and 'dying', and the protagonist himself becomes imaginatively entangled with inhuman entity of the 'black hole'. [*AO1 for advancing the argument with judiciously selected quotes; AO2 for close language analysis*]

- Although the outcomes of their acts of resistance and rebellion are starkly different, both poems nevertheless explore the aftermath of challenges to oppressive forces, and the struggle involved in inspiring change.

Conclusion:

'Dharker's 'A Century Later' and Femi's 'Thirteen' both delve into themes of rebellion and resistance amidst the backdrop of contemporary socio-political issues. By drawing upon their unique perspectives and experiences, Dharker and Femi illuminate the enduring resilience and defiance of their protagonists. By invoking the real-life struggles of Malala Yousafzai and the broader issues associated with the Black Lives Matter movement, the poems provide a rich and insightful exploration of the power of resistance and rebellion in challenging oppressive forces and effecting change. As such, these works serve as an important testament to the human spirit's capacity to endure and fight for justice, even within the most challenging of circumstances.'

A Black Lives Matter protest in the aftermath of George Floyd's murder.

ESSAY PLAN FIVE
'LIKE AN HEIRESS' & 'HOMING'

Pollution on a Caribbean beach, reminiscent of the detritus Grace Nichols's speaker encounters. We have opted not to reproduce Nichols's poem in full: it is still in copyright and we wish to respect that fact.

Compare the ways in which the poets present ideas of change in 'Like an Heiress'

by Grace Nichols and one other poem from Worlds and Lives.

Introduction:

'Nichols's 'Like an Heiress' and Berry's 'Homing' both delve into the personal impact of change upon individuals, as they grapple with the shifting sands of personal and cultural identity. Though hailing from quite distinctive cultural and historical backgrounds – Nichols's poem originates from the Caribbean, while Berry's stems from the UK's Black Country – both poets confront the personal implications of change and the longing for connection with their past. In Nichols's poem, the physical environment reflects the changes occurring in the narrator's emotional connection to their childhood home. In contrast, Berry's poem focuses on the impact of societal expectation on the erasure of a regional accent and, consequently, the individual's connection to their heritage.'

Theme/Paragraph One: Both poems explore the theme of loss due to change. In Nichols's poem, the landscape has been tarnished; in Berry's poem, it is the speaker's mother's accent that has been eroded.

- In 'Like an Heiress,' Nichols laments the sweeping aftermath of environmental change on the narrator's homeland, strikingly pictured through the vivid imagery of 'the lone wave of rubbish...plastic bottles...styrene cups.' This jarring depiction of a tarnished seascape serves to intriguingly amplify the narrator's poignant sense of lost connection to her birthplace. The list of waste items cast upon the beach, notably inanimate and unnatural, starkly contrasts with the organic serenity typically associated with Caribbean landscapes, thereby underscoring the harshness and alienating impact of pollution. Moreover, the phrase 'lonely wave of rubbish' encapsulates the narrator's sense of abandonment and alienation in witnessing the trashing of her once pristine surroundings – the rubbish, like the narrator, is lonely, cast out, and out of place. This could perhaps reflect Nichols's concern about the adverse implications of rampant globalisation and unregulated tourism on the Caribbean.[1] [*AO1 for advancing the argument with judiciously selected quotes; AO2 for analysis of language and in-depth exploration of imagery; AO3 for associating the poem's themes with Nichols's personal background and the broader socio-environment mishaps*]

- Pivot to comparison: In 'Homing,' Berry addresses the British historical context and societal pressures leading individuals like the speaker's mother to stifle aspects of their regional identity, such as their accent: 'For years you kept your accent in a box beneath the bed...the teacher's ruler across your legs.' The trochaic metre employed by Berry here emphasises the speaker's mother's compliance with societal expectations and subtly conveys her internal struggle to suppress her regional dialect and adhere to standard English.[2] [*AO1 for advancing the argument with a judiciously selected quote; AO2 for discussing how form shapes meaning; AO3 for situating the poem in the historical context of regional stigma in the UK*][3]

Theme/Paragraph Two: Both poems explore the idea of memory as a source of strength amid change.

- In 'Like an Heiress,' Nichols skilfully employs metaphors to emphasise the profound personal connection the speaker retains with her past, despite the disquieting panorama of environmental degradation. The metaphorical expression 'oceanic small days' alludes to the narrator's heartening memories of her childhood, instilling a sense of longing to re-embrace the halcyon days of unspoiled nature.[4] The phrase 'oceanic small days' could be read as an oxymoron: the term 'oceanic' connotes vastness and depth, whereas 'small days' implies a reduction or diminution, perhaps reflecting the narrator's nostalgia for a diminished past.[5] Also, the reference to the 'sun' as 'the only eldorado,' suggests that the warming, golden tone of the sun might symbolise reminiscences of a 'golden' era prior to the transformative impacts of pollution observed. [*AO1 for advancing the argument with a judiciously selected quote; AO2 for close language analysis*]
- <u>*Pivot to comparison*</u>: Equally, in 'Homing,' Berry employs a rich palette of nostalgic language to explore the speaker's longing to revive her eroded regional dialect and heritage. The speaker's resolve to 'swallow

them all,' in reference to the words and phrases tied closely with the Black Country, highlights a consuming desire to internalise and become one with the lost aspects of her cultural identity. Each element that the speaker wishes to take in — 'the pits, railways, factories' — offers a snapshot of the Industrial Revolution, thereby evoking a tangible link to the region's storied past. Furthermore, this is crystallised by the architectural metaphor of the 'red brick back-to-back,' a characteristic housing style of the Black Country during the Industrial era. [*AO1 for advancing the argument with a judiciously selected quote; AO2 for discussing how structure and language shape meaning; AO3 for relating Berry's literary technique to the broader historical context of the UK*]

Theme/Paragraph Three: The use of a single, reflective perspective characterises both poems, emphasising the internal struggle presented by change.

- Nichols's 'Like an Heiress,' employs a first-person narrative, allowing readers to experience the protagonist's intimate emotional landscape and their struggle with the rapid environmental transformation. For instance, the phrase 'I stand and gaze' captures the introspective, contemplative tone of the poem, emphasising the solitary journey of the speaker as they navigate their altered homeland. Similarly, Nichols's use of emotive language in 'like a tourist, I head back,' captures the protagonist's feeling of displacement and alienation whilst 'brooding' and contemplating deeply on the perils of change in the 'air-conditioned darkness.' These words and phrases work in concert to shed light on the protagonist's internal turmoil as they encounter and grapple with the stark changes to their once familiar environment. [*AO1 for advancing the argument with judiciously selected quotes; AO2 for analysing the specific language use; AO3 for relating the individual experience depicted in the poem to the larger context of environmental concerns*]

- <u>*Pivot to comparison*</u>: In contrast, 'Homing' articulates the struggle to preserve regional culture through Berry's deliberate choice of dialect and form, employing the first-person narrative perspective to accentuate the intimacy and emotional depth evoked by the speaker's quest for her mother's suppressed identity. The free verse structure of Berry's poem provides ample space for these fluid shifts in language and cultural references, further complementing the poem's themes.[6] Additionally, Berry's use of hyperbole, as seen in the expression 'I wanted to swallow them all: the pits, railways, factories...' powerfully captures the speaker's longing for connection to their heritage and emphasises the significance of maintaining those ties despite societal pressure to conform to standard English [*AO1 for advancing the argument with a judiciously selected quote; AO2 for discussing how the form shapes meaning; AO3 for relating Berry's literary technique to the broader context of UK regional identity*]

Conclusion:

To wrap things up, I am going to invoke a third poem – one that is in fact not included in the anthology – to demonstrate contextual knowledge beyond merely commenting on historical circumstances (and thus score some bonus AO3 marks). I shall then use it as a means to tie up my argument...

> 'Reflecting on the implications of climate change for future generations, John Agard's 'Inheritance' – released alongside Nichols's 'Like an Heiress' in the same 2015 RSA Climate Change anthology – poignantly asks: 'Should we dance or break into gnashing of teeth at the news of our inheritance?' This questioning sentiment resonates with the explorations of transformation presented in both Nichols's 'Like an Heiress' and Berry's 'Homing.' Each poem, while rooted in uniquely distinct geographical and cultural contexts, navigates the emotional terrain of displacement and the individual quest for resilience. The richness of these narratives lies not only in their nuanced depictions of change, but also in their potent affirmation of retaining connections to heritage and roots amidst societal or environmental upheaval.'

ESSAY PLAN SIX
'ENGLAND IN 1819' & 'IN A LONDON DRAWINGROOM'

England in 1819
By Percy Bysshe Shelley

An old, mad, blind, despised, and dying King;
Princes, the dregs of their dull race, who flow
Through public scorn,—mud from a muddy spring;
Rulers who neither see nor feel nor know,
But leechlike to their fainting country cling
Till they drop, blind in blood, without a blow.
A people starved and stabbed in th' untilled field;
An army, whom liberticide and prey
Makes as a two-edged sword to all who wield;
Golden and sanguine laws which tempt and slay;
Religion Christless, Godless—a book sealed;
A senate, Time's worst statute, unrepealed—
Are graves from which a glorious Phantom may
Burst, to illumine our tempestuous day.

Introduction:

____

'George Eliot's mid-nineteenth-century poem 'In a London Drawingroom' and Percy Shelley's politically charged sonnet 'England in 1819' are united in their critiques of the expectations and norms that govern their respective societies. Both poems were written in the context of significant social and political changes in nineteenth-century England. While Eliot's poem focuses on the urban numbness of London life, Shelley's work takes a more direct approach, launching a scathing attack on the political landscape of England in his day. Both poets offer a bleak outlook on the state of society, drawing from their respective experiences and the broader historical context of their time.'

Theme/Paragraph One: Both poets suggest that the societal norms at work are oppressive, stifling creativity and life itself.

- In 'In a London Drawingroom,' Eliot describes the suffocating urban environment of Victorian London, with the sky 'yellowed by the smoke' and 'the houses opposite / Cutting the sky with one long line of wall.' The metaphor of the houses 'cutting' can be seen as an aggressive intrusion of these man-made structures into the natural world, while the line break just before 'Cutting' emphasises the violence of this verb. This reflects the historical context of the rapidly expanding city during the Industrial Revolution, as increasing urbanisation led to worsening air quality, congestion, and social disconnection. [*AO1 for advancing the argument with a judiciously selected quote; AO2 or close language analysis and discussing how form shapes meaning; AO3 for providing historical context*]

- Eliot also presents a bleak scene devoid of life and natural beauty, stating that, 'no bird can make a shadow as it flies' and that people in the streets 'glance unmarking at the passers-by.' There is a sense that nature and individuality have been erased from the urban consciousness, reflecting the societal norms of a rapidly industrialising society. [*AO1 for advancing the argument with a judiciously selected quote*]
- Pivot to comparison: Like Eliot, Shelley criticises the norms governing society in 'England in 1819,' though he focuses on the broad national setting rather than the urban. Shelley portrays a society acquiescing to dire conditions, writing of 'A people starved and stabbed in th' untilled field.'[1] This phrase is laden with powerful, emotive language. Shelley's choice of the words 'starved' and 'stabbed' depict a population subjected to extreme suffering, highlighting the cruelty and apathy of societal expectations. Moreover, the image of the 'untilled field' uses agricultural symbolism to suggest both neglect and wasted potential. [*AO1 for advancing the argument with a judiciously selected quote; AO2 for close language analysis*]
- Shelley's bleak picture, then, resonates with the sense of urban desolation that Eliot paints in 'In a London Drawingroom,' with both poets condemning the societal norms that allow such conditions to persist.

Theme/Paragraph Two: Both poets critique oppressive systems governing their societies, highlighting the need for change.

- In 'In a London Drawingroom,' Eliot's urban setting is described as 'one huge prison-house & court / Where men are punished at the slightest cost, / With lowest rate of colour, warmth & joy.' The metaphor of a prison suggests that rigid societal norms and expectations keep people trapped in a cycle of disconnection and apathy. Eliot employs anapestic meter in these lines, which consists of two unstressed syllables followed by a stressed syllable (e.g., 'one huge pris-'). This rhythm contributes to the sense of confinement and monotony by creating a uniform beat that mirrors the oppressive sameness of the urban environment. This critique echoes the work of contemporaneous author Charles Dickens, who similarly condemned the oppressive nature of Victorian society, particularly urban life, in works such as 'Oliver Twist' and 'Bleak House.' [*AO1 for advancing the argument with a judiciously selected quote; AO2 for discussing scansion; AO3 for referencing a contemporaneous author*]
- <u>*Pivot to comparison*</u>: In 'England in 1819,' Shelley takes a more direct approach, slamming the rulers of the time as 'blind in blood, without a blow.' Shelley criticises the ruling class further by using potent metaphors, describing these individuals as 'Princes, the dregs of their dull race, who flow / Through public scorn—mud from a muddy spring.' By painting the ruling class as akin to 'dregs' and 'mud,' Shelley underscores corruption and decay, reflecting the climate of social unrest and calls for political reform prevalent in 1819 England. Thus, Shelley does not merely critique the ruling class's blindness to systemic

issues but also takes aim at their moral and political corruption. This moral and political corruption was perhaps best encapsulated by the infamous Peterloo Massacre of 1819, where the government brutally suppressed peaceful protestors.[2] [*AO1 for advancing the argument with a judiciously selected quote; AO2 for discussing the use of metaphor; AO3 for providing historical and socio-political context*]

Theme/Paragraph Three: In both 'In a London Drawingroom' and 'England in 1819,' societal norms are critiqued, but while Eliot suggests resignation, Shelley envisions revolutionary change.

- While 'In a London Drawingroom' vividly outlines the dour conditions of urban life, Eliot refrains from explicitly propounding a vision for change or resistance.[3] Through her depiction of individuals absorbed in their mundane tasks, as they 'All hurry on & look upon the ground,' Eliot suggests a resigned acceptance of societal norms rather than active defiance. The downward gaze serves as a metaphor for defeat or compliance, implying that the inhabitants have been forced into submission. Interestingly, the poem's markedly regular structure, with consistent rhyme scheme and metre, further echoes this narrative of monotonous routine and conformity, thereby reinforcing the bleak depiction of societal norms. [*AO1 for advancing the argument with a judiciously selected quote; AO2 for discussing how structure shapes the argument*]

- *Pivot to comparison*: In contrast, Shelley's 'England in 1819' concludes with a burst of optimism as he envisions 'graves from which a glorious Phantom may / Burst, to illumine our tempestuous day.' This evocative image of a radiant spirit emerging from gloom encapsulates a potent vision of revolutionary change, reflective of the disruptive spirit of the Romantic era. This sentiment echoes the revolutionary potential found in contemporaneous literature, such as Blake's 'The Tyger,' where a fierce creature – often interpreted as a symbol of revolution – is celebrated.[4] Thus, like Blake, Shelley sought to challenge societal norms and envision a transformative future. [*AO1 for advancing the argument with a judiciously selected quote; AO3 for providing historical and contextual links to contemporaneous literature*]

Conclusion:

'Eliot's 'In a London Drawingroom' and Shelley's 'England in 1819' present a critique of societal norms, spotlighting the oppressive systems curtailing life and creativity. Eliot mirrors the surrender to urban conformity, offering a portrait of resignation rather than hopeful rebellion. Conversely, Shelley tackles power structures head-on, envisioning potential revolutionary change. Thus, the two poets engage with societal norms from different vantage points, one resigned and one revolutionary.'

Percy Bysshe Shelley.

Percy Shelley was one of the most influential voices of the Romantic movement.

ESSAY PLAN SEVEN

'POT' & 'A WIDER VIEW'

Mesopotamian pots displayed in the British Museum. We have opted not to reproduce Khan's poem in full: it is still in copyright and we wish to respect that fact.

How do the poets convey the importance of personal history and heritage in 'pot' by Shamshad Khan and one other poem from Worlds and Lives?

Introduction

I have chosen to focus on 'pot' by Shamshad Khan and 'A Wider View' by Seni Seneviratne because both poems delve into the intricacies of personal history and heritage.

> 'Despite their vastly different styles and historical contexts, both Shamshad Khan's 'pot' and Seni Seneviratne's 'A Wider View' delve into themes of personal history and heritage. Khan's 'pot,' written in the early 21st century, reflects the complex issue of cultural displacement in the context of globalisation and post-colonial identity. Conversely, Seneviratne's 'A Wider View' is situated in the context of 19th-century England, chronicling her great-great-grandfather's personal history amidst the harsh industrial landscape. Though these poems are separated by time and cultural milieu, the shared themes of displacement, the power of narrative, and the malleability of identity emerge as common threads.'[1]

Theme/Paragraph One: Both 'pot' and 'A Wider View' wrestle with the experience of being displaced from one's cultural and historical context, leading to a heightened awareness of personal history and heritage.

- In 'pot,' the persona the speaker addresses is a fragile pottery artefact displaced from its homeland and held in a foreign collection. Khan illustrates the pot's precarious condition in lines such as 'so fragile you might break' and 'someone somewhere will have missed you.' This displacement underscores the importance of heritage and personal history, as the pot becomes a symbol for the diaspora experience, reflecting the post-colonial struggle for identity — it is both a literal pot, but also a stand-in for the proverbial displaced person.[2] Khan's use of free verse, characterised by its lack of rhyme scheme and varying line lengths, symbolises the instability and fluidity associated with diaspora and displacement. The irregular structure of the poem reflects the lack of order and control the pot possesses over its own narrative, thus further reinforcing the instability of its identity. [*AO1 for advancing the argument with judiciously selected quotes; AO2 for close language analysis and for discussing how structure shapes meaning; AO3 for placing the poem in historical context*]

- <u>*Pivot to comparison*</u>: In 'A Wider View,' Seneviratne similarly explores the displacement of her great-great-grandfather from his native Sri Lanka to Leeds, England, where he sought better opportunities for his family amidst an oppressive industrial environment. His search for 'spaces in the smoke-filled sky to stack his dreams,' with its use of alliteration echoing his ceaseless aspirations, points to a longing for ties to his heritage even as he erects a new existence in a foreign land. The poet's meticulous description of the setting, such as 'Marshall's Temple Mill' and 'Tower Works,' showcases the historical landscape of 19th-century industrial Leeds, grounding the poem in a specific timeline. [*AO1 for advancing the argument with a judiciously selected quote; AO2 for close language analysis; AO3 for detailed historical context*]

- While both poems, then, showcase the struggles of displaced individuals, they each provide unique perspectives on the concept. 'pot' provides a contemporary and seemingly metaphorical portrayal of cultural displacement, whereas 'A Wider View' is an attempt to vicariously understand the displacement of an older family member. [*AO1 for advancing the argument with relevant comparisons*]

Theme/Paragraph Two: Both poems emphasise the importance of storytelling in reclaiming heritage and personal history.

- Khan's piece calls for the pot to 'tell me the rest' of its story, showcasing the importance of narrative in piecing together one's heritage. The pot's uncertain history is depicted through a series of speculations and unanswered questions, mirroring the experience of diaspora communities seeking to reconnect with their cultural roots. The poet's use of free verse and anaphora creates a sense of urgency and longing for the pot's story to be unveiled. Moreover, Khan's scansion choices contribute to the poem's rhythm, with the occasional use of iambic pentameter, as in 'tell me the rest, pot / of how you got here', which reinforces the interrogative nature of the poem and adds emphasis to the protagonist's desire for answers to her queries about heritage. [*AO1 for advancing the argument with judiciously selected quotes; AO2 for analysing the poet's use of language, form, and scansion*]

- *Pivot to comparison*: In 'A Wider View,' Seneviratne vividly chronicles her great-great-grandfather's experiences assimilating into a foreign society in lines such as 'eyes dry with dust from twelve hours combing flax beneath the conicals of light in Marshall's Temple Mill.' This meticulous attention to detail serves as a narrative reclamation of her family's personal history. Moreover, the depiction of her ancestor's longing for a 'wider view' serves as a metaphor for the longing to bridge the gap between past and present, heritage and newfound identity. Through phrases such as 'the long way home' and 'the comfort of a wider view,' Seneviratne seamlessly weaves together two disparate cultural worlds, speaking to the power of storytelling in unearthing and preserving one's roots. The narrative is not just a recount of the past, but an active re-experiencing and preservation of a deeply personal narrative [*AO1 for advancing the argument with judiciously selected quotes; AO2 for analysing the poet's use of language*]
- Both 'pot' and 'A Wider View' shed light on the power of narrative as a tool for exploring personal history and heritage, but they utilise different methods to do so. 'pot' implements a conversational tone, and free verse to create an urgent, questioning energy, reflecting a present-day search for cultural roots. On the other hand, 'A Wider View' employs a more detailed, descriptive storytelling style that portrays a lineage narrative existing within the past's fabric and the present's context. [*AO1 for relevant comparison*]

Theme/Paragraph Three: Both poems explore the fluid nature of identity in the process of reconnecting with one's heritage.

- In 'pot,' Khan's speaker explores the idea of the pot being from 'anywhere' and 'almost an English pot,' showing the pot's struggle to assimilate into its new environment. The poet uses synecdoche to emphasise the fluidity of identity, with the pot standing for the larger experience of cultural displacement. The lines 'someone/somewhere/will have missed you pot' showcase the personal history and heritage of the pot becoming a metaphor for the cultural loss experienced by diaspora communities. Additionally, the use of repetition and rhetorical questions underscores these conflicting cultural forces that contribute to the malleability of identity.[3] [*AO1 for advancing the argument with judiciously selected quotes; AO2 for analysing the use of language techniques and discussing synecdoche*]
- <u>*Pivot to comparison*</u>: Seneviratne's 'A Wider View' also navigates the malleability of identity, as her great-great-grandfather finds solace in Giotto's 'geometric lines' — an allusion to the Renaissance painter's innovative techniques that were revolutionary at their time.[4] This appreciation of art and its transcendence of cultural boundaries represent a merging of differing identities, highlighting the fluidity of personal heritage and history.[5] [*AO3 for discussing historical context*]

Conclusion

I often like to read interviews with poets – not only can they give you insights into the way they think, but citing these interviews can also help you score crucial AO3 marks: after all, they show that you have been reading around your subject!

'Seni Seneviratne, in a 2011 interview with *Barely South Review*, argued that poets strive to give their narratives a 'texture, so a reader can feel it.' This perfectly encapsulates the exploration of displacement, narrative power, and fluid identity in Khan's 'pot' and Seneviratne's 'A Wider View.' Both works convey that personal history and heritage are rich, multifaceted human experiences uniquely felt by each individual – a sentiment effectively grounded in their respective historical contexts.[6] Thus, the poets do more than tell; they enable readers to feel the complexities of personal history and heritage in a profoundly emotive way.'

ESSAY PLAN EIGHT
'IN A LONDON DRAWINGROOM' & 'THE JEWELLERY MAKER'

In a London Drawingroom
By George Eliot

The sky is cloudy, yellowed by the smoke.
For view there are the houses opposite
Cutting the sky with one long line of wall
Like solid fog: far as the eye can stretch
Monotony of surface & of form
Without a break to hang a guess upon.
No bird can make a shadow as it flies,
For all is shadow, as in ways o'erhung
By thickest canvass, where the golden rays
Are clothed in hemp. No figure lingering
Pauses to feed the hunger of the eye
Or rest a little on the lap of life.
All hurry on & look upon the ground,
Or glance unmarking at the passers by
The wheels are hurrying too, cabs, carriages
All closed, in multiplied identity.

The world seems one huge prison-house & court
Where men are punished at the slightest cost,
With lowest rate of colour, warmth & joy.

Explore the ways in which poets explores the relationship between humanity and its environment in George Eliot 'In a London Drawingroom' and one other poem from Worlds and Lives.

Introduction

For this essay, I have decided to compare Eliot's 'In a London Drawingroom' to Louisa Adjoa Parker's 'The Jewellery Maker.' Since they were written at very different points in time, I will start the essay by placing both pieces in context – and, in the process, will score early AO3 marks. I shall then signpost where my thematic argument is headed, so the examiner can start seeing where I'm planning to pick up my AO1 marks.

'Though distinct in their styles, George Eliot's pre-Raphaelite critique of urban life and Louisa Adjoa Parker's contemporary, free-verse narration intersect in their exploration of humanity's relations with their environments.[1] Eliot's 'In a London Drawingroom' paints a stark and grim portrait of urban monotone, encapsulating the inhabitants within a homogeneous, oppressive urban malaise.[2] In contrast, Parker's 'The Jewellery Maker' celebrates the harmonious dance between a rural craftsman and his natural surroundings, revelling in the vibrant rhythm of this symbiosis.'[3]

Theme/Paragraph One: Both poets explore the relationship between individuals and their surroundings, albeit in contrasting ways. Parker uses the jewellery maker to exemplify a harmonious human-nature bond, while Eliot sharply portrays human detachment from the natural world in an urban setting.

- In Parker's 'The Jewellery Maker,' the protagonist's lifestyle harmonises with the daily rhythm of nature, an aspect indicated when he begins his tasks 'each day after sunrise.' This cyclical phrase echoes the sun's predictable journey, underlining the natural synchronisation between the artisan and his environment. Within this constructive dialogue, the craftsman shapes elements from nature into artistic expressions — manifesting as 'gold butterflies,' 'flowers,' and 'silvery moons.' Here, the poet employs metaphorical transformations to highlight how human creativity can mirror and augment natural beauty. [*AO1 for advancing the argument with a judiciously selected quote; AO2 for close language analysis and discussing how form shapes meaning*]
- <u>*Pivot to comparison*</u>: Eliot's sharp critique of urban life presents a stark tension between humanity and its environment. The repetition of unvarying, regular iambs in lines like, 'The world seems one huge prison-house & court' purposefully mimics the relentless

monotony of urban existence, subtly echoing the monotonous urban environment – a physical manifestation of the stark 'Monotony of surface and of form / Without a break to hang a guess upon.' In addition to the landscape, inhabitants, too, appear suppressed, enclosed within a cityscape marked by multiplied, identical identities: 'all closed, in multiplied identity.' Such a lack of distinct metrical variation, like the homogeneity noted among its urban dwellers, reinforces Eliot's theme of brutal uniformity in a typically Victorian urban existence. Thus Eliot cleverly employs form, structure, and scansion to further emphasise her critique of such an oppressive, conflict-ridden urban environment. [*AO2 for language analysis, and discussing how form and structure—at a metrical level—shapes meaning; AO3 for placing the work in a historical context*]

Theme/Paragraph Two: Both poets present the ways in which their environments shape not only individuals but also the nature of their interactions and relationships. Parker portrays an environment conducive for personal contentment and social harmony. In contrast, Eliot's urban setting seems to create isolation and anonymity, reinforcing a sense of social disconnection.

- Parker's poem illustrates an idyllic setting where the jewellery maker interacts harmoniously with his surroundings, his craft, and his community. His relationship with the social environment is reflected in the congenial greeting of his neighbours: he 'greets his neighbours with a smile,' suggesting a sociability and openness indicative of a close-knit society evoked through such simple yet significant moments of shared humanity. The warmth in his social interactions underscores the conduciveness of his environment to communal cohesion. [*AO1 for advancing the argument with a judiciously selected quote; AO2 or close language analysis and discussing how form shapes meaning*]

- This genial sociability is not confined to friendly exchanges outside; he translates his heartfelt affection to his wife in the intimate domain of married life. His humble confession of how he would 'drape his wife in fine-spun gold' reveals a deep admiration for her. His affection gets artistically embodied when he imagines the 'unlined skin' of potential female customers 'warming the metal his hands caress.' In this scenario, gold, warmed by the jewellery maker's affectionate touch, is presented as an extension of his love — his art. [*AO1 for advancing the argument with a judiciously selected quote; AO2 for the close analysis of the language*]
- <u>*Pivot to comparison*</u>: On the other hand, in Eliot's urban environment, monotony and confinement serve to stifle human interaction. 'All hurry on & look upon the ground,' communicates the lack of meaningful social interaction with city dwellers displaying an indistinct, almost robotic demeanour as they 'glance unmarking at the passers by.'
- Notably, the use of the word 'unmarking' here could be viewed as a powerful linguistic echo of William Blake's depiction of urban life in his poem 'London'. Blake uses the term 'marks' to imprint signs of

'weakness' and 'woe' on every face, indicating a city permeated by despair. This paints a picture of an urban populace burdened by sorrow, reflecting the gloomy societal landscape charted by Eliot. However, the 'unmarking' of Eliot's Londoners implies a disengagement or withdrawal from their environment and each other, as opposed to the active suffering implied by Blake's 'marks.' This further highlights Eliot's critique of urban existence as a space of detached anonymity where vibrant human connections are eroded by the oppressive urban life. [*AO1 for advancing the argument with a judiciously selected quote; AO2 for close language analysis; AO3 for drawing a connection between two texts and providing wider poetic context*]

Theme/Paragraph Three: The poets uniquely explore individuals' power or agency within their environment. Parker's protagonist creates artefacts, directly impacting and interacting with his environment, while Eliot's characters are resigned to polite suffering in their urban prison-like environment.

- Through the figure of the jewellery maker, Parker emphasises that individuals have the capacity and power to interact positively with their environment. The words 'he likes hot metal, the smell, the way it yields to his touch' detail the maker's active engagement with his materials. Indeed, Parker shows that man's agency can extract and mould raw elements into creative expressions of beauty that embody nature's rhythm — 'Under deft fingers gold butterflies dance.' The Jewellery Maker is not only a passive observer but a proactive contributor to his environment, consequently adding to local cultural traditions with his craft. [*AO1 for advancing the argument with a judiciously selected quote; AO2 for close language analysis*]

- Pivot to comparison: In contrast, Eliot's urban dwellers appear to have little agency over their existence — they appear incapable of escaping their oppressive habitat. This is reinforced by the phrase 'No bird can make a shadow as it flies, / For all is shadow.' The typically freeing act of a bird in flight is drained of its usual sense of liberty and movement, instead becoming swallowed in the urban gloom and thus signifying the shackling of freedom inherent in her cityscape. Eliot's metropolis becomes an urban 'prison-house,' imprisoning its seemingly powerless dwellers. The unsettling phrase 'all is shadow' conjures an image of pervasive gloom, using the metaphor of the shadow to convey a sense of tangible engulfment and echoes the confinement denoted by the 'prison-house' analogy. Together, they starkly capture the urban dwellers' loss of individual agency, dictated to by their inhospitable surroundings. [*AO1 for advancing the argument with judiciously selected quotes; AO2 for close language analysis*]

Conclusion

'Parker, in her 2019 essay 'At the Water's Edge', meditates on the transformative power of one's environment, stating that 'being in coastal spaces helps me accept my life.' This principle resonates in her poem, where the jewellery maker, though in a different environment, finds harmony and purpose in his surroundings. This stands in stark contrast to the alienated inhabitants of Eliot's metropolis, who are depicted as trapped within their oppressive cityscape.'

A portrait of George Eliot.

NOTES

ESSAY PLAN ONE

1. Dichotomy refers to a division or contrast between two things that are represented as being opposing or entirely different.
2. An iambic tetrameter is a type of metrical line used in traditional English poetry and verse drama. Let's take a step back and talk about what makes up an iambic tetrameter by discussing Shakespeare and iambic pentameter.

   Many students would have heard of the phrase 'iambic pentameter' when studying texts such as Shakespeare's plays. The first word, 'iamb', refers to a metrical foot in poetry. The second word, 'pentameter', means that there are five metrical feet in the line.

   For instance, if we took a line from Shakespeare's Romeo and Juliet and marked out each metrical foot with a vertical line and highlighted the stressed syllables, it might look like this: 'In **fair** | Ve**ro**| na, **where** | we **lay** | our **scene**.'

   Each metrical foot consists of two consecutive syllables, and there are five metrical feet in total, hence the term pentameter. The stress in each metrical foot is on the second syllable, making the foot an iamb.

   Now, when we talk about iambic tetrameter, we are referring to a metrical line that only has four iambs instead of five; the 'tetra' in tetrameter means four. Each iamb still consists of two syllables, but there are only four of these metrical feet per line.

   This gives the lines in an iambic tetrameter a rhythmic pulse, producing a steady and flowing rhythm. This metrical structure allows the words to flow gently, similar to the natural rhythm of speech, which can draw readers into the emotional resonance of the poem.
3. Metonym is a figure of speech in which a thing or concept is referred to by the name of something closely associated with that thing or concept.
4. Pantheism refers to the belief that the natural world is itself a physical incarnation of God.
5. Maori: The indigenous Polynesian people of New Zealand. The speaker in 'With Birds You're Never Lonely' encounters a Maori woman during his visit to the Zealandia forest, providing an opportunity for cross-cultural learning and understanding.
6. Ambivalence refers to the state of having mixed feelings or contradictory ideas about something or someone. In the conclusion, the term refers to Antrobus' mixed feelings towards his hearing aids.

ESSAY PLAN TWO

1. The interlocutor is the individual to whom a narrator is talking.
2. A figure of speech in which a part is made to represent the whole or vice versa. For example, calling a car 'wheels' is a type of synecdoche because the wheels are part of the car. The difference to metonymy lies in this part-whole relationship - metonymy doesn't keep this relationship but uses something closely related or associated as a substitute.
3. Anaphora refers to a literary and rhetorical device in which a word or group of words is repeated at the beginning of two or more lines, clauses, or sentences.
4. A clarion call is a strongly expressed demand or request for action. In this context, it refers to the call for reconnection to nature.
5. Oscillation means moving or swinging back and forth at a regular speed.
6. Enjambment refers to the continuation of a sentence without a pause beyond the end of a line, couplet, or stanza.
7. Precariousness refers to the quality of being uncertain or unstable.
8. Ethereal means extremely delicate and light in a way that seems not to be of this world.
9. Celestial refers to the sky or visible heaven, or to the universe.
10. Hyperbole refers to exaggerated statements or claims not meant to be taken literally.

    Magnanimity refers to the fact or condition of being magnanimous; generosity.

ESSAY PLAN THREE

1. Juxtaposition refers to the fact of two things being seen or placed close together with contrasting effect.
2. An anapestic foot is a metrical foot in poetry that consists of two short syllables followed by one long syllable (or two unstressed syllables followed by one stressed syllable).

ESSAY PLAN FOUR

1. The Ku Klux Klan (KKK) is an American white supremacist hate group whose primary targets are African Americans, along with Jews, immigrants, leftists, and, until recently, Catholics. The KKK has existed in three distinct waves at different points in time during the history of the United States.
2. Malala Yousafzai a Pakistani activist known for staunch advocacy for girls' education. Her international prominence rose when, at 15, she survived an

assassination attempt by the Taliban in 2012 after publicly campaigning against the group's attempts to restrict girls' education in her region.

Following her recovery, Malala continued her activism at a global scale, resulting in her becoming the youngest recipient of the Nobel Peace Prize at the age of 17 in 2014.

3. Spondees refers to a metrical foot consisting of two stressed syllables.
4. The Taliban is a fundamentalist Islamist group primarily located in Afghanistan and Pakistan.The group emerged in the early 1990s during the turmoil in Afghanistan following the withdrawal of Soviet troops and the ensuing civil war. The Taliban sought to establish a theocratic state, governed by their strict interpretation of Islamic law (Sharia). They controlled Afghanistan from 1996 until 2001, when a U.S.-led invasion toppled the regime. However, following the U.S. withdrawal from Afghanistan in 2021, the Taliban reestablished control over the country.

   The group is known for their harsh enforcement of their interpretation of Islamic law, including restrictions on women's rights, and for their destruction of cultural monuments.
5. George Floyd was a Black man who died in the Powderhorn community of Minneapolis, Minnesota on May 25, 2020 after Derek Chauvin, a white police officer, knelt on Floyd's neck for about nine minutes during an arrest.

   Floyd's death triggered widespread protests around the world, demanding justice for him and many others who died as a result of police brutality, and calling for an end to systemic racism.

   Video footage of Floyd's death quickly went viral and became a symbol of the Black Lives Matter movement. Chauvin was convicted of murder and manslaughter in April 2021.
6. Autobiographical: Of or relating to a person's life or an account of a person's life, as told by the person themselves.
7. Meta-fictionality refers to a form of fiction that emphasises its own constructedness in a way that continually reminds the reader to be aware that they are reading a work of fiction.

ESSAY PLAN FIVE

1. Globalisation refers to the process by which businesses or other organisations develop international influence or start operating on an international scale.
2. A dialect is a particular form of a language that is peculiar to a specific region or social group. Dialect is an integral part of regional identity which, when suppressed, can lead to an erasure of cultural identity.
3. Stigma refers to a mark of disgrace associated with a particular circumstance, quality, or person. In this essay, it refers to the negative perception and treatment associated with regional accents in the UK.

4. Halcyon refers to a period of time in the past that was idyllically happy and peaceful. In the poem 'Like an Heiress,' the phrase 'halcyon days' is used to recall a time before the environmental degradation occurred.
5. An oxymoron is a figure of speech in which apparently contradictory terms appear in conjunction. Here, 'oceanic small days' may seem a contradiction, as 'oceanic' often refers to vastness, while 'small days' suggests diminution.
6. Free Verse is a form of poetry that does not rhyme or have a regular rhythm.

ESSAY PLAN SIX

1. Acquiescing means passively accepting or going along with something.
2. Peterloo Massacre took place on August 16, 1819 in Manchester, when cavalry charged into a peaceful crowd of about 60,000 people who had gathered to demand political reform and better representation in Parliament.

   This disastrous event left an estimated 15 people dead and hundreds injured. It marked a pivotal moment in the struggle for democratic reform in the UK, sparking public outrage and eventually leading to significant changes in UK laws and rights for the working class.
3. To propound is to put forward an idea or theory for consideration by others.
4. Contemporaneous means occurring or existing in the same period of time.

ESSAY PLAN SEVEN

1. Malleability refers to the quality of something that can be shaped into something else without breaking, in this context, used metaphorically to indicate the ability to adapt or be changed.
2. Diaspora refers to the dispersion or spread of any people from their original homeland.
3. A rhetorical question is a question asked in order to create a dramatic effect or to make a point rather than to get an answer.
4. Born around 1267, Giotto di Bondone, commonly known as Giotto, was an Italian painter and architect from Florence in the late Middle Ages. He is generally considered the first in a line of great artists who contributed to the Italian Renaissance.
5. Transcendence refers to existence or experience beyond the normal or physical level.
6. To be multifaceted is to have many facets or aspects.

ESSAY PLAN EIGHT

1. Pre-Raphaelite refers to a style of art and literature popular in the mid-19th century. Characterized by detailed observation of the natural world and complex compositions, its followers believed in an art of serious themes and meticulous techniques.
2. Monotone refers to the quality of having one unvarying tone; lacking in variation and dynamism.

   To be homogeneous is to be of the same or a similar kind or nature.
3. Symbiosis refers to a closely associated, mutually beneficial relationship between different types of organisms or things.

Printed in Great Britain
by Amazon

37126570R00047